Following Your Steps

FRANCES MORALES

WestBow
PRESS
A DIVISION OF THOMAS NELSON

WestBow Press books may be ordered through booksellers or by contacting:

WestBow Press

A Division of Thomas Nelson

1663 Liberty Drive

Bloomington, IN 47403

www.westbowpress.com

1-(866) 928-1240

Because of the dynamic nature of the Internet, any web addresses or links contained in this book may have changed since publication and may no longer be valid. The views expressed in this work are solely those of the author and do not necessarily reflect the views of the publisher, and the publisher hereby disclaims any responsibility for them. Any people depicted in stock imagery provided by Thinkstock are models, and such images are being used for illustrative purposes only. Certain stock imagery © Thinkstock.

ISBN: 978-1-4497-7995-5 (sc)

ISBN: 978-1-4497-7994-8 (e)

ISBN: 978-1-4497-7996-2 (hc)

Library of Congress Control Number: 2012923855

Scriptures taken from the Holy Bible, New International Version®, NIV®. Copyright © 1973, 1978, 1984, 2011 by Biblica, Inc.™ Used by permission of Zondervan. All rights reserved worldwide. www.zondervan.com The "NIV" and "New International Version" are trademarks registered in the United States Patent and Trademark Office by Biblica, Inc.™ Scripture quotations marked (NIV) are taken from the Holy Bible, New International Version®, NIV®. Copyright © 1973, 1978, 1984, 2011 by Biblica, Inc.™ Used by permission of Zondervan. All rights reserved worldwide. www.zondervan.com The "NIV" and "New International Version" are trademarks registered in the United States Patent and Trademark Office by Biblica, Inc.™ All scripture quotations, unless otherwise indicated, are taken from the Holy Bible, New International Version®, NIV®. Copyright ©1973, 1978, 1984, 2011 by Biblica, Inc.™ Used by permission of Zondervan. All rights reserved worldwide. www.zondervan. com The "NIV" and "New International Version" are trademarks registered in the United States Patent and Trademark Office by Biblica, Inc.™. All rights reserved.

Printed in the United States of America

WestBow Press rev. date: 1/14/2013

Dedication

To my loving husband, Danny, God's faithful and obedient servant!

For over forty years, I have witnessed your love and faithfulness to the Lord's work. Your passion for souls has inspired me during all these years. Danny, you have been an exemplary minister as well as a faithful and loving husband and father. Your children respect and honor you.

You are the fountain of joy in our family. Because of you, our hearts have been full of laughter and joy. Each joke or anecdote is unique and special because no one can tell it like you. Your family is thankful for all the years you have blessed us with unending joy and laughter. Through the long years of your ministry, the Lord has given you an abundance of spiritual children in different countries that love and admire you.

I dedicate this book of memories to you, with all my love. I know you will never seek fame, glory, or acknowledgment. Humbleness is one of your most precious qualities. May these memories be a blessing for our children, grandchildren, family, friends, and our brothers in the Faith so they will glorify the name of God who called us and is forever Faithful. Blessed be the name of our Lord.

I pray that after people read this book, many will embrace and follow the calling of the Lord like you have and be able to walk in His footsteps.

With love, your wife,

Frances

Contents

Dedication v

Foreword ix

Acknowledgments xi

Introduction xiii

Chapter 1: A Calling 1

Chapter 2: I Will Go! 3

Chapter 3: A Family 11

Chapter 4: Facing Death 17

Chapter 5: Knowing the God of All Consolation 23

Chapter 6: Avance Misionero's Plan in Honduras 41

Chapter 7: 1980 Honduras' Year 51

Chapter 8: Helping God 55

Chapter 9: Living by Faith 57

Chapter 10: Enlarge the Place of Your Tent 65

Chapter 11: Leaving Footprints 71

Chapter 12: Thank You, Dad 83

Chapter 13: You Will Leave More Footprints 87

Appendix 1 89

Appendix 2 91

Appendix 3 93

Foreword

Anyone who knows Pastor Danny Morales must agree with me that he is the epitome of faith in action. He is very optimistic and always has a smile on his face. He shares his good humor. However, this doesn't hinder him from depending on the Holy Scriptures to give advice at the right moment.

His radio program, *Cántaros de Bendición: Pitchers of Blessing*, in which I had the opportunity to participate, is a good example of what I mentioned before. It is an application of God's Word to the daily needs of the radio listeners. The book you have in your hand, *Following Your Steps*, describes the character and testimony of Pastor Morales through his wife's pen. It is a refreshing work. When you read it, you will feel as if you are talking to him, and the influence of this godly man will touch your life.

Every chapter has experiences, and when you read these, you will feel in your heart the desire to get closer to that loving God that Pastor Danny serves. The main purpose of this book is to encourage anyone who is considering embracing the ministry so that you may trust the God who brother Danny has served. He has provided for all of Danny's needs. It is a living testimony that God gives us talent, the opportunity, the finances, and the anointing to serve Him.

I have had fellowship with Pastor Morales for many years, and I haven't seen in him change like shifting shadows. I say this to support this book. Pastor Danny Morales is a man who in times of emergencies and natural disasters in different countries is always ready to lend a helping hand, serving as a bridge between the needy people and those who are willing to support his ministry. He is constantly travelling to different countries in Latin America and the United States in order to hold youth and marriage retreats. He also provides retreats for the pastors and their wives. They receive Bible teachings, counseling, books, and training to encourage them to keep serving God.

I believe that as you see this profile of my dear partner in the ministry, you will appreciate this literary work and will be thankful I recommended it to you. For you, dear brother Danny, my sincere congratulations. I will see you at the CVS LA VOZ Radio Station's kitchen to laugh or to cry.

Sincerely,

Dr. Juan Romero

Preacher, composer, singer

Acknowledgments

First, foremost and always, I would like to thank God for the honor and privilege of writing this book. I am grateful for the help and support of the following individuals.

- Danny for your testimony and service to the Lord.

- My children, who have encouraged me to write.

- Dr. Juan Romero for his love, friendship, and the blessing of writing the Foreword.

- Julian Kuilan and my sister, Luz for the long hours spent reading and typing the manuscript.

- My daughters, Rebecca and Liza for their assistance with the translation and corrections.

- DeAnn Marx; Elise Angiolillo; Gabriel Meruelo; and Alfonso Orellana, who read, edited and/or translated this manuscript.

Introduction

I began writing this book four years ago to share God's faithfulness during my husband's, Daniel Morales, forty years in the ministry. God led him to do things that were not in Danny's plans for the future.

I would like these memories to be a message of encouragement to those who have been called to work as pastors, evangelists, missionaries, teachers, or laypeople. These memories are real. We lived them, and we are thankful to our God for the privilege He gave us to serve Him. I believe with all my heart that the Lord always supports those He has called to serve Him.

In each chapter, you will find testimonies of God's greatness and faithfulness. It is my prayer that you will be touched by the Holy Spirit in such a way that if you need encouragement to begin your ministry, your faith will grow when you see how God has blessed His servant, Danny. If you are working in the ministry, may you keep going strong, knowing that your labor in the Lord is not in vain. Remember, there are many servants around the world who bravely continue to proclaim that Christ died to save mankind. If God called you a long time ago and you didn't embrace that call, get on your knees and tell God, "Here I am. Send me like you sent brother Danny." Maybe you were called to clean the temple, sing, teach, or work with children. Believe me, any work we do for our God is important for Him. So lift up your heart and serve God. Seize the day!

Chapter 1: A Calling

In December 1968 during a prayer meeting, a group of students from the University of Puerto Rico was called by the Lord to go to the mission field in many different countries. One of those students was Danny Morales. He was called to go to Honduras. The Lord spoke to Danny and said, "I need you in Honduras." The Lord told this young man that he would not finish college and would instead travel to many places. Danny was in his second year of college, attending the Catholic University in Bayamón, Puerto Rico. This calling changed his life completely. He had planned to finish a degree in accounting, buy a boat and a house, marry me, and start a family.

However, God had other plans and spoke to his heart in such a way that Danny was able to leave everything. He believed that God was calling him to serve in the mission field. Even when he received hurtful criticism, Danny embraced his calling and believed with all his heart that God had truly called him to His service. Even though some did not believe that Danny's calling was real, Danny did not dismay and decided to serve the Lord.

During a Bible study, Sister Judith Román de Santos, after she heard about Danny's calling, asked God in prayer why He had called Danny, who was still a spiritual baby. God answered her, "I have called many who have attended Bible institutes, and they have not accepted the call. They are sitting in their churches. I know Danny will obey." Unanswered questions still remained. Why, Danny, Genoveva's only son? Soon, the answer came: "Did not I send my only son to die for man?"

She continued searching for an answer and asked, "Lord, they are such a small group of students. How are they going to sustain themselves as missionaries?"

The Lord replied, "Their families will help them." There was silence and no more questions to God. It was clear that He had called Danny and would look after him.

Through praying and fasting, Danny started getting ready to leave with the support of the small group of students, who gave offerings and tithes from their allowances. The group brought travel tickets for Danny and two other young students. They were so excited that they sold postcards, baked cakes, and even painted garbage cans for the community in order to raise the funds needed.

They planned their trip as the Lord revealed it to them, and they left for Honduras in July 1970. Reverend Luis Rivera from the Christ Missionary Church of Honduras was willing to help them and receive them in his home until they could establish themselves.

Chapter 2: I Will Go!

Then I heard the voice of the Lord saying, "Whom shall I send?
And who will go for us?" And I said, "Here am I, Send me!"
(Isaiah 6:8)

To this calling, Danny responded, "I will go Lord, send me". He left the beautiful island of Puerto Rico on July 12, 1970, on Pan American Flight 456 at 1:30 p.m. He was barely nineteen years old, with his Bible in his hand and a one-way ticket to the Republic of Honduras. With a heart full of passion for saving lost souls, Danny left his family and girlfriend.

Judith Santiago and Gabriel Alvarez accompanied him. Danny was very happy dressed in style with a new suit. That night, they stayed in Miami and arrived at San Pedro Sula [1]the next day. From there, they went with Reverend Luis Rivera to another city called Siguatepeque[2].

As they traveled through the green and fertile Valley of Sula, they became homesick for their beloved island. However, their joy of

---

1   City in Northern Honduras

2   City in Central Honduras

obedience to the missionary calling kept their hearts light, and they began to admire the high Honduran mountains.

They journey was rough once the paved roads were gone. Only dirt roads full of stones and holes met them until they arrived at Siguatepeque. This is how their adventure began, and it changed their lives forever. Every time the truck hit a ditch, the new missionaries' heads would hit the roof, but you could only hear them worshipping and blessing the Lord. Clouds of dust fell on the excited passengers as the group traveled through the dirt roads.

Nothing deterred the new missionaries from talking, laughing, and singing as they continued their journey. After long hours of travel, at midnight they finally arrived, all covered in dust, tired, hungry, and thirsty. His suit was covered with dust, and the only food available was black coffee and bread. Danny did not drink coffee. Exhausted, they spent their first night on the mission field, but they were still very happy. They were in Honduras!

In addition to the warm welcome that Reverend Luis Rivera and his family gave them, nature gave them a special welcome. In the morning, a very dense fog fell upon the city of Siguatepeque on the mountain plateau.

At dawn, very large birds with open wings posed on the patio. They were turkey vultures. Danny was very excited and called his companions to come and see the birds. They had never seen birds that big, and they all ran into the house from fear of an attack. It was just turkey vultures taking an early morning a sunbath.

When they walked to the church at night, they heard the scary gloomy song of many large frogs that sounded like moaning ghosts. But nothing stopped their walk. All three of them ignored their fears and joyfully arrived at the church.

The first Saturday after Danny's arrival, he was chosen to be the youth convention preacher. From the first moment he learned that he was going to preach, he began to fast because his nerves would not allow him to eat. That Saturday, his message was this: "I have heard about you, but today, my eyes can see you." He preached for about fifteen minutes and then gave an altar call. He was amazed that all the youth came forward! Some were reconciled, and others gave their lives to Christ Jesus, our Lord.

As the youth came to the altar, Danny was on his knees, overwhelmed with joy about what was happening in that church. The Lord touched the hearts of the youth and confirmed that Danny and his companion missionaries had truly been called to the ministry at the same time. They knew that they had the Lord's support.

Danny's joyful character helped him make friends quickly. He touched many lives, and numerous people came to the Lord as he continued to preach the Word in the city of Siguatepeque. One time when he got excited during his preaching, a woman heard Danny say, "Wow, wow," and assumed he was barking. After the service, she said, "It is a shame. He preaches so beautifully, but he barks!" That was when he was labeled as the barking preacher.

As time passed, the Honduran hospitality changed Danny's food preferences, and he learned to drink coffee and eat tortillas, beans, and other different foods instead of his usual rice, beans, and fried pork chops from Puerto Rico.

Although, Honduras is a Spanish-speaking country, Danny had to learn the region's dialect. He began to call the children *cipotes* instead of *niños* (children) and used *ahorita* instead of *ahora* (now) to state the urgency of things. He also had to stop using specific words that had bad connotations and were offensive in Honduras.

An Evangelist's First Steps

Danny's first evangelistic crusade lasted one week in Taulabé[3], a village by the Yojoa Lake. He never forgot the daily menu of small red beans, *frijoles*, eggs, and corn tortillas for breakfast, lunch, and dinner. Although he had a new diet and had to go into the bush for his sanitary needs, Danny came home happy. He continued glorifying the Lord because so many souls had received Christ as their personal Savior and because he had learned to eat Honduran food.

After a few months, he was sent to San Pedro Sula to establish the Christ Mission Church. He was alone in a city that he did not know, and he had no friends. He lived in a small room and started his missionary work around the small bars located at the end of Cabanas neighborhood. God answered his prayers. Little by little, people began to come, and the church began to grow.

In order to sleep, he had to bend his canvas cot behind the door and move two benches. His guitar and Bible were his companions. Many times, he cried from loneliness during his meals. He was used to living with a joyful family and had a hard time learning how to live alone. He quickly learned how to iron his clothes, cook, and keep his new home in order.

---

3   Village near Lake Yojoa

Memories from San Pedro Sula

One day, a man walked toward the altar while Danny was preaching. At that moment, Danny thought, *Oh, Lord, what is that man going to do to me?* To his surprise, the man took out a knife and said, "Pastor, take this knife. I was going to kill my wife and children, but when I passed by and heard your message, I changed my mind. I want you to pray for me." That day, God saved a family, and the man started going to church with his wife and children.

Call unto Me and I Shall Answer

It was a very joyful day, one that missionaries call a fat cow day. Danny was very excited he was going to cook his favorite food pork chops. He hurried to put the chops in the frying pan and lit the stove. He was amazed to find that the burner's fire was dwindling because of the lack of gas. He was sad and prayed, "Oh, dear Lord, not today. Don't let the gas be out today." He shook the small gas tank from side to side and tried to start the fire once again without success. He started to imagine how his dinner would consist of bread and water. Then he began to pray to God for a miracle, for he was very hungry. He said, "Lord, I am hungry, and I don't have gas for the stove. I need a miracle." And the Lord heard his prayer. When he tried to start the stove again, a fire sparked immediately. Those pork chops were delicious, and the gas for the stove lasted a whole month.

A Giant against David

One afternoon, a tall man who was standing in front of the church began insulting Danny. Neighbors surrounded the man. Suddenly, the man moved toward Danny. The courageous missionary closed his eyes and raised his hand to heaven in prayer, expecting the giant man to break him into small pieces. Closing his eyes was absurd, but an angel of the Lord protected him. Danny was astonished because he did not feel the expected hit, only heard the sound of a body falling to the ground. Immediately, he heard the neighbors saying, "He killed him." When Danny opened his eyes, he saw that the man had fallen and looked like a boxer who had been knocked out.

How did the Lord do it? Danny did not know, but he suddenly started to think about how this story was going to make the front page of the newspaper tomorrow morning. The paper would probably say, "Puerto Rican missionary kills a Honduran man." He was very scared. He got close to the man and began to pray that the Lord would raise him. After a little while, the man got up and left. After that day, no one in the neighborhood challenged the missionary.

Encounter with a Guatemalan Guerilla

One night, Danny held a home Bible study in San Pedro Sula. He was teaching the parable of the Samaritan woman when a young man suddenly fell on his knees and started crying. Danny came closer and prayed for the young man, and that individual accepted Christ as his personal savior.

Afterwards, the young man testified that he was fleeing from Guatemala and that his cousin had invited him to the Bible study. When he entered the house and saw Danny (who was about 128 pounds at that time) he thought, *what could this boy teach me? I am a guerrilla,*[4] *a man of weapons and fights.* He testified that when Danny was teaching, his thoughts were interrupted when he saw Jesus standing behind Danny, and that's when he fell on his knees to the floor. After his experience of salvation, his life changed drastically. He left his riffle behind and began carrying a Bible. Today, he is a pastor!

---

4   See testimony to the guerrilla in Appendix 1.

The Glory of Obedience

Over the forty years of Danny's ministry, I have seen the Lord beside him. Hundreds of souls have been won to Christ, and many lives have been restored. All the fruits of this ministry are the Lord's for His honor and glory.

Last week, my daughter, Rebecca, said to me, "Mom, where would all the souls that you and Dad have won for the Lord be if you and Dad had not obeyed the Lord when He called you?"

My eyes filled with tears, I said, "Becky, there is glory in obeying." Danny and I have never regretted obeying the Lord's call. He has always been faithful and never abandoned us.

We have reaped roses for God, and sometimes thorns in the path have caused pain. But today, we have a beautiful bouquet of roses that we can place at the Lord's feet for His honor and glory. We have served the Lord, who has called us. We are His servants, and all the glory is for Him.

I truly believe that Danny and every missionary that obeyed the call to go to Honduras has been blessed and can sing the hymn[5] "The Glory of Obedience." There is no greater glory on earth than obedience to the Lord.

---

5   Hymn written by Pastor Ramón Nieves.

Chapter 3: A Family

"Our dreams are divine, but they would be more divine if they became a reality. That is why I ask you, my love, that we never stop loving each other." Danny wrote these verses to me when we were dating.

With those words, he said goodbye to me in 1970. For a year, we maintained the flame of our love through letters because there was no e-mail and calling was very expensive. A year later, I arrived at the town of Siguatepeque to work with the missionaries, Luis Rivera, and his beloved wife, Marcelina. In that beautiful town, we exchanged vows on September 5, 1971.

I cannot forget that Danny, with his funny disposition, said, "Now that I am married, the Honduran girls have scratched my name off their lists." We moved to San Pedro Sula, where Danny was ministering at the Christ Missionary Church. There, the Lord blessed us, and we enjoyed our first year of ministry. Our congregation was small but beautiful.

In 1972, the following year, we stopped working with the Christ Missionary Church and moved to the city of Comayagua. We went to that city because God had indicated to Danny that He wanted him preaching there. With a lot of excitement, we began working in the area, founded our own mission, and gained missionaries like Rubén Nieves, Judith Santiago, and Gabriel Alvarez. We called the mission Avance Misionero en Honduras, and we soon completed all of the paperwork to incorporate the mission with the government.

I remember while I was pregnant with my first baby, we did not have a dinning table, chairs, or living room furniture. To eat, I would sit on the step between the kitchen and the living room. One day, Danny arrived with some pieces of wood, nails, a hammer, and a chair that a neighbor let him borrow. To my surprise, my loving husband became a carpenter and started making a table so that I would not have to eat while I was sitting on the floor anymore.

We traveled to Puerto Rico and stayed there for a few months. On June 20, 1972, God blessed us with a beautiful daughter whom we named Rebecca. The firstborn of the family, she miraculously survived, although she was born prematurely and only weighed four and a half pounds. In the midst of the happiness and excitement of being parents, the doctors told us that we should prepare ourselves for the worst because they did not believe that our little girl would survive. In one instant, our happiness was snuffed out, and it became sadness and uncertainty. Danny tried to comfort me with all his love, and during the night as we held hands through tears and sobs, we cried out to God for our baby. We both remembered months before that God had given us a message: "Frances, blessed is the fruit of your womb." Filled with faith, we put Rebecca in the Lord's hands, and fifteen days later, she was sent home from the hospital.

Now our baby doll, as we lovingly call her, is married to Michael Moore. They have two beautiful children, Victoria Jean Moore and David Michael Lawrence Moore. Currently they reside in Cleveland, Georgia.

On August 18, 1973, God added to our family another beautiful and very special girl named Frances Beatriz. During that time, we returned from Puerto Rico and went to Comayagua. My *puchi*, as I lovingly call her, is married to Brian McQueary, and they live in Louisville, Kentucky, with their beautiful sons Alexander Scott, Breyton Rey, and Cameron. Their other son, Tyler Enrique, who was Breyton's twin brother, went to be with the Lord when he was less than a month old.

I wrote these verses for my beloved Becky and Frances when I invited them to ask Jesus into their tender hearts:

> There are two little stars,
> Their light is now shining
> Because in their heart
> Lives the Redeemer (1975).

> My two little stars have
> Inside of them
> Your love and your grace
> That one day you gave them.
> Thank you, Lord.

My two little missionaries grew up surrounded not only by our love but also the love of the brothers and sisters of Honduras and the missionaries that came from Puerto Rico. They played with their uncles Rubén Nieves, Ramón Nieves, Gabriel Álvarez, their aunts Judith Santiago, Felícita Pérez, Ana M. Hernández, Lucy

Nieves, Gladys Pérez, Nelly Westerband, and Milagros Chervoni, and they spoiled them.

Four years later, the Lord blessed us with another baby. "Maybe this time, we will have a boy," we said with great excitement. When we gave the news of my pregnancy to the congregation, they began praying for a boy. The Lord answered that prayer on June 5, 1976, when our gorgeous and long-awaited son was born in Comayagua. We named him David Daniel. Someone put up a sign in front of the church that said, "Danny had a boy," and everyone celebrated the arrival of David Daniel.

I was so overwhelmed with happiness that I wrote these verses to David Daniel:

> Wonder from heaven,
> When I felt in my womb
> The heartbeat of a little one,
> I asked Thee, Oh God (May 1976).

> David Daniel has arrived,
> A very special little boy
> I would love to cry out
> God is faithful.
> He heard my prayer.
> Thank you, Lord (June 1976).

Our happiness did not last long. At five and a half months, David Daniel was called to his heavenly home. (See Chapter 4: Facing Death.)

Two years after David Daniel's death, we asked the Lord for another child. He heard us and answered our prayer and on April

4, 1978, when Daniel Isaiah was born in the city of Comayagua. He was a beautiful baby. I called him my prince. We called the house where all the missionaries lived the "Missionary House." It was a house filled with joy and happiness again. Every day, people stopped by with presents to congratulate us. Little Danny filled our home with happiness.

I wrote Daniel Isaiah these verses:

> Son, asked of the Lord,
> You brought a message from heaven
> To comfort our hearts
> You are special, a long-awaited son,
> A son loved and desired.
> You are the answer from God.
> Like Ana dedicated Samuel,
> I consecrate you for God.
> Be faithful to God, Daniel.

Daniel Isaiah currently lives in Alabama with is wife, Nicole Morales, and their beautiful daughter, Sofia Nicole. Our son is a police officer, and he preaches in various churches.

At the end of 1978, we went to Puerto Rico, where we spent two years studying the Word and spending time with Danny's mom. She was very ill with breast cancer. We praise the Lord because in the midst of her sickness, she accepted Christ and got ready to one day be with Him.

While we were in Puerto Rico, God blessed our lives once again, and on February 24, 1980, our beautiful daughter, Liza Raquel, was born. She came to our house and filled it with love and joy. I call her my baby because she is the baby of the family. She lives in Florida with her husband, Jason Popour, and their daughter, Natalia Isabella. I also wrote a poem to Liza:

> You are my little piece of heaven,
> A gift from God
> You fill my life with love
> You are sweet and loving.
> Whoever you meet, you bless with your love.
> Every smile, every word wraps us with your love.
> Thank you, Liza, for your love.

Chapter 4: Facing Death

One would like to be prepared to encounter death, but death arrives without notice. In the most unexpected moment, we receive news that one of our loved ones, a friend, or an acquaintance has just died. When this happens, we are taken by surprise. It amazes us, and many times, it makes us think that one day, we might die as well.

When our minds start thinking, *I will die one day*, this makes us shudder down to our cores. Immediately, we disregard the thought, saying to ourselves, "I am too young to die. I should not think about death." After the mourning period for the loved one is over, we no longer think about death until it comes knocking at the doors of our homes once again.

As believers, we prepare ourselves to encounter death with our faith. Jesus said, "I am the resurrection and the life. The one who believes in me will live, even though they die" (John 11:25). As servants of the Lord, we are not exempt from facing death, and like every human being, we have to face it. But this time, it was on the mission field.

During the Christmas holiday of 1974, two of our missionaries from Puerto Rico visited us. They were on their way back to Nicaragua. Their names were Nelson Cordero and Moisés Avilés. On the afternoon of New Year's Eve, a friend of ours invited them to go for an outing in a river close by. They were very excited to accept the invitation not knowing that one of them would die by drowning in the waters of the Humuya River in Comayagua. Moisés, Jr., drowned that day. Immediately, the sad news reached the Missionary House. Once again, were touched by the horrible knock of death at our door. For us, those moments felt as if time stood still. The missionaries were in shock. Some cried, and others just shook their heads back and forth in disbelief and said, "It can't be true."

As a missionary group, we had to confront the death of one of our own just as we were preparing to celebrate the last day of the year with a church service and dinner at midnight. It was not easy. The sadness was overwhelming, and we had to turn our eyes to the God of all consolation. That night, the service was one of intercessory prayer for the Avilés family. We asked God to comfort these parents who had sent their only son to the mission field.

The town of Comayagua showed their love and stood by us in our pain. Friends and neighbors and fellow Christians came to the house to pay their respects. We had to send the body to Puerto Rico. We did not have money or transportation, but once again, God used Carlos Yuja, who lent us the money we needed as well as his truck.

At midnight that day, Danny arrived at the capital of Honduras with the body of the young missionary to make arrangements with the funeral home to transport the body to Puerto Rico. Because it was New Year's Day, people in the capital were celebrating with firecrackers, fireworks, lights, and music while Danny and the men who accompanied him were enveloped in a veil of mourning because of the death of their friend, Moisés. It was a very difficult time for Danny. As director of the mission, he assumed his responsibility, and with his broken heart, he travelled to Puerto Rico to give the parents of the young man his body.

Death Knocks at the Door of My Heart

One day, our baby, David Daniel became gravely ill. He was only five months and three weeks old. I took him to the hospital and when they were treating him, he went into cardiac arrest. After much effort, they could not revive him. As I saw my son dying, I closed my eyes and asked God for strength. My little one died at one o'clock in the afternoon on October 26, 1976.

Soon after, my beloved missionaries and some friends and members of our church came to comfort me and gave me strength with their love. That day, I was by myself because Danny was in San Pedro Sula.[68] He had gone there to comfort Sister Pacita Zacapa because her husband had just died. That afternoon, Danny arrived, and with profound pain, he hugged the lifeless body of little David. In that moment, my heart broke even more, seeing my dead baby and his father crying over him. At that precise moment of so much pain, the Lord sent His servants Reverend Felix Montes, a Puerto Rican missionary from the Pentecostal Church, Reverend Ruben Vargas another Puerto Rican missionary from the Assemblies of God Church, and other pastors to our house. They interceded for us and surrounded us with their love.

---

6   [8] San Pedro Sula city to the north of Comayagua (approximately three hours away)

After they prayed, Danny hugged me and cried and sobbed. Later on, he locked himself in the bathroom, and there, he asked God for strength. At that very moment, the Lord filled him, and the Holy Spirit comforted him. A little while later, he came out of the bathroom to comfort me and said, "Tonight, we will have a worship service to our God." Our good friend and partner in the ministry, Reverend Ruben Vargas, lovingly led the praise and worship service. That night, Danny told the congregation, "Brethren, next to me is my dead son, and my God is worthy of all praise. I will worship Him at all times. Even in this moment in which I am confronting death so closely, I praise Him."

The Saturday before David's death, Danny had raised his hand when the missionary Arquímides Rivera had preached on Psalm 34:1 and had asked that those who were willing to praise God at all times to raise their hands. How quickly Danny had to put into practice what he had promised in front of his congregation!

That night, instead of having a sad viewing, we had a night of worship. Something totally out of the ordinary happened. Instead of people comforting us, Danny comforted the men, and I comforted the women, all of whom were crying for our son. Every hug that they gave us, every tear that we saw, and their love filled us with blessings in order to go through this trial.

Someone brought me pills for my nerves, but I did not need them. The Holy Spirit was in control. My heart was covered with something I cannot explain. How did this happen? There was only one answer. The God of all consolation had comforted us, and that is how we were able to comfort so many brothers and sisters on that night.

A few days later, a young maid came to my house with snacks from my neighbor, Mrs. Blanquita Henríquez. She sent me a message that she wanted to speak to me. I went to her house to drink coffee, and with a lot of love and sorrow, she gave me her condolences for the death of my son.

During our conversation, she told me, "Frances, I was there the night of the viewing, and I was amazed to see how you and Danny were the ones comforting the people instead of them comforting you. I saw such peace in you. Please tell me what is it that you have that I don't have."

I answered, "We have Christ in our hearts, and we have experienced God's consolation. Our son is with God." Then she said, "I want what you have."

That day, my dear neighbor opened her heart so that Christ would come into her life. This was confirmation that when God manifests in the midst of our pain and trials, other lives receive blessings.

After the death of David, we went to Nicaragua for a few days, and when we returned, Danny preached at the Central Church in Comayagua. You will read the message in the next few pages. I pray, dear reader, that you will be blessed through this message.

Chapter 5: Knowing the God of All Consolation

November 1976, Danny preached this message to the Church in Comayagua, Honduras based on II Corinthians 1:3-6. "We have a God that is so great. He has given us the spirit of life. This spirit of life is what we have received, and that is why life is what we possess in Christ Jesus. It does not matter if there are valleys with dried bones. God has the power to form the flesh, the nerves, the tendons, and He even has the power to call on His spirit to give these things life. And one day, dear brothers and sisters, among those bones He will raise the bones of David, and he will be formed again in flesh and taken to the heavenly kingdom.

Beloved, the Lord has truly comforted us, and God's comfort is amazing. And tonight, I am going to talk to you about precisely that, the Consolation of God. I invite you to open your Bibles and look at Second Epistle of Corinthians chapter one, starting with the third verse.

Not too long ago, I was talking about these verses at the Bible Institute, and truthfully, when we were studying these verses, they were, shall we say like a theory. But God allowed me to put them into practice.

The Word of God acquires such a great value for life when it has been put to work in our lives. That is when we begin to see marvelous things and can begin to savor how powerful the Word of our God is.

After the death of my son, I asked God why He allowed David's death. I did not ask why He let him die or why He did not intervene, but I wanted to know why He allowed him to die. What did God want to teach us? What did God want us to understand? What was the purpose for this happening?

We studied in the book of Job that even though he experienced so many bad things, Job did not blame God. He knew that God had a purpose for everything that had happened, even though he did not understand it. What was God's real purpose? Job knew that God was in control. I know that my God has a purpose, and I want to understand it so that I can then, like Job, who when he looked back at what had happened, said it was all worth it. I want to be able to look back one day and say it was all worth it and I will have understood God's purpose.

In these verses that I found in 2 Corinthians, God has given me a purpose. God has already shown me why He allowed this to happen. Dear brothers and sisters, we do not have a more truthful word than the Word of God, and this Word has taught me why He has allowed this suffering. The Apostle Paul begins by saying, "Praise be to the Lord God and Father of our Lord Jesus Christ." He begins with praise. This is amazing, seeing how the Apostle Paul worships, even though he had been through tribulations, many afflictions, hunger and on many occasions had been left for dead. Paul tells us in Thessalonians, namely that we need to give thanks in all things, something that is even more difficult to understand. This is very strange—that he would begin the theme about afflictions, tribulations, and needs by giving praise before anything else.

You can ask me, "How can I give thanks for the death of a person? How can I give thanks to God for the people who are dying of hunger? How can I give thanks for those who are sick? How can I give thanks for those people who are suffering from horrible diseases?" Of course we cannot give thanks for those things. What Paul teaches us is that even though we cannot give thanks for everything that is happening, we can give thanks to God because even though things may be happening, He is with us no matter what. This means that it does not matter how bad the circumstances are, God never leaves us. And this is a reason to rejoice and a reason to give thanks to our God at all times.

It is easy to have religion when everything is going well, but my dear brethren, sometimes when we have to give up our lives for that religion, it is easy to say, "I don't belong to them. I am no longer with that religion." When a person said to Peter, "You also were with Jesus of Galilee," Peter replied, "I don't know him." That was the critical moment for Peter, a very difficult moment. It was the moment when his life was at stake, and Peter did not have enough faith. He did not have a true belief, and he preferred to lie. There are many people who go inside their homes, hide, and don't come to the house of the Lord when the moment of trial comes. They don't dare enter His temple because they are not sure of what they believe when hard times come.

There was a man who said he had built a shield that was bulletproof, and he went to the general and said, "I have created this bulletproof shield." The general did not pay much attention to him, and the man said, "This will be phenomenal for our army. Anyone can put this shield on, and not one bullet will penetrate it."

The general said, "You put it on first and see how it fits." Then he ordered a soldier to shoot the man in the chest. The man immediately took off the shield. The shield was not as good as he had said, and he was not sure that it would save his life.

Brothers and sisters, maybe the biggest test of faith lies in how we are going to respond in times of trial, how we will respond in the presence of God and in the eyes of the world in the midst of our trials. Will we begin to curse things? "Curse God and die," Job's wife said to him.

He replied, "You are talking like a foolish woman, even if you ask me to curse Him, I will continue to bless the name of my God." Beloved, what a faith! What stability! What temperance this man had in the presence of the Lord! When we are faced with trials, what will we say? And when the trials are overwhelming, what will we do? Will we continue serving Him? Will we continue blessing God? Will we give God continual praise? Will we bless Jesus at all times?

We can give thanks to God at all times because He has given us the strength, the hope, and the faith so that we can bless Him in the moments of affliction and trial. This shows us several things. Among them is this: the heart of a man that praises God in the midst of trials and affliction is not defeated to the point of killing the soul with desperation. And that, at the moment of affliction, that person can raise his or her hands and praise God, even in the middle of the storm just like Paul and Silas praised God when they were in jail with their backs bleeding because of the whippings they had received. It was midnight then, and they had not been given even coffee. They were in a dark cell because many people did not even want to know about them. But the Lord did know about them, and when they began to pray and sing hymns, the earth began to tremble. The doors to the cells were opened, and their chains felt off.

When bad things happen to us, these things tend to stop us in our tracks. When you have a problem with someone and this person always comes back with a bad response and all of the sudden, you say, "I am sorry if I offended you," in that moment, that person will be in shock because he or she will not be expecting that response.

I remember that when I was a little boy and wanted to go out with my mom, she would tell me no. I would throw a fit, cry, and scream. Then she would always leave me at home. One day, my mom said to me, "You are not going," and she was ready to give me the speech of the century when I responded by saying that it was okay. That day, my mom put me in her car and took me with her.

That is why the earth had to tremble at one point because it was not expecting the response of those two who were praising God in that moment. The earth had to move because the earth was waiting for them to curse and for the guards to kill them. When the earth heard them begin to sing, the angels in the sky also heard them singing. When the Lord heard their song, which was coming out of affliction, He made the earth tremble.

When we bless God in the midst of our afflictions, Paul and Silas's experience shows that there is hope. Hope, the Bible itself says, is not ashamed. Hope is life. I see hope as something that encourages us and gives us strength. When we are encouraged, we have life. One can see amazing things happen when in the middle of tribulations, we praise God.

During a soccer game, when the score is two to zero. What happens to the team that is losing? The team feels discouraged. The players begin to lose interest in playing, and that is when the other team scores another eight goals, winning ten to zero. This occurs because the team is discouraged, and the players lose the hope to win. But if the team that is losing has the hope of winning, the players will keep fighting. They feel encouraged and continue playing, even though they are losing. In the Christian life, the Christian that feels beat up and that feels like the trials in their life are tearing his or her soul apart has to know that there is still hope, which is why the Christians do not stop and will not be defeated.

Listen to me. Even though we may be crushed and we are placed in a tomb with a shovel or whatever it is, from there, we will arise with the sound of the trumpet. Our God is great! Christ has given us the most glorious hope, the greatest promise: "I am the resurrection and the life. The one who believes in me will live, even though they die" (John 11:25). Hallelujah!

With this hope, what else would we want on earth? The thing that man is worried the most about is death. God has taken away death. "Oh, death, where is your sting? Oh, grave, where is your victory?" said the Apostle Paul (1 Corinthians 15:55). In Christ, we have won! When God speaks about the Christians that are dead in Christ, he says that they are sleeping. In 1 Corinthians 15:6, it says, "After that, he appeared to more than five hundred of the brothers at the same time, most of whom are still living, though some have fallen asleep."

When God talks about those who are already asleep, He is talking about those who have already departed. The Lord speaks about sleeping and how sleeping is a natural act because all of us sleep. God tells the Christian child, "Don't worry because you will not die. You are going to rest." Once we have lived our lives here, where we are pilgrims, and have said with our own mouths that this is not our home, well, brothers, when things here end, then we will be there in our heavenly home.

Scientists that study the body say that sleep is where we grow and where we regain our strength. If God says that when we leave this world, we will be asleep, and when we wake in Christ, we will be restored. One day, we will awaken full of life, abundant life to never sleep again. What a beautiful promise from God!

He is the Father of compassion and the God of all comfort (II Corinthians 1:3). This means that yes, He is the God of all comfort and compassion. Will there be anything that happens to us that God will not have the power to comfort? No, there will not be an affliction He will not comfort. There will not be a tribulation that would annul the fact that God is the God of all consolation. Praise God!

No, dear friends, no single trial is superior to the ability He has to comfort us. He does know how to comfort us. What do people run to for comfort? When the moment of death or a time of trial comes, some find comfort in friends to counsel them, to cry with them, to encourage them to keep going. There are others who act differently and run toward sin when trials come. If their moms die, they run to drink alcohol for months to forget their sorrow, to forget that they have lost loved ones. Others will resort to using drugs to be in a state of imaginary wellbeing in order to forget what has really happened.

Dear friends, the hope of God takes us to the very presence of God. How beautiful is our Lord! The comfort of God helps us to praise him in the midst of trials. A Christian that believes in the Word of God and has believed in Christ receives His comfort.

Once, there was a minister who had a friend who was on his deathbed, and the man of God asked his friend, "How are you feeling today?"

And he said, "I feel as if my head is resting on three soft pillows— the first, infinite power; the second, infinite love; and the third, infinite wisdom. Infinite power because if there are bones that God wants to raise, He will raise them. Infinite love because what God allows is greater. Infinite wisdom because what God knows is beyond all mortal comprehension. Hallelujah!"

Do you believe that God does things out of order? God never does things out of order. God has a plan and a purpose that is beautiful because what God does is beautiful. "God saw all that he had made, and it was very good" (Genesis 1:31a). God still sees everything He is doing as good. In that is our confidence and hope.

What does our comfort consist of? In Psalm 119:49–50, the psalmist said something beautiful about where my comfort is: "Remember your word to your servant, for you have given me hope. My comfort in my suffering is this: Your promise preserves my life." Where is the comfort? The comfort is in God's Word.

Let's look at the Word, Romans 15:4 reads "For everything that was written in the past was written to teach us, so that through endurance and the encouragement of the Scriptures we might have hope". There are moments that are so sad, so traumatic in which the Scriptures give us the comfort we need. Only one drop of God's Word that falls upon our hearts can inundate us and comfort us. People who have believed God's Word have obtained life, and through that very same Word, their life is sustained. He comforts us in all of our tribulations and trials. There is not a trial that God cannot comfort because the Word tells us that in all things, we will be comforted. God is not a liar. In all tribulations and trials, He will comfort us.

Why will He comfort us? One reason why God took my son was so that we could then comfort those who were going through any trial or tribulation. Through the comfort that we have received from Him, we can be comforters. He does not comfort us so that we go to the hurting and say, "I have also been through trials, and my heart broke in two pieces. And my heart cried, and I suffered for two months." It is not for us to identify with the trials of others. We suffer so that we can then comfort anyone who is suffering through the comfort we have received.

It is not that I can compare my trial with yours but that when I see your pain compared to mine, I can then say to you that God has comforted me. God's consolation has come to my life so that in the midst of trials you can also say, "Just like God was with the Morales family, I know He will be with me." You can then have someone to lean on. Trials and tests will come at very difficult times. The Bible does not tell us that the days will get better; it tells us that days will get worse. Beloved friends, get ready so that when difficult times come, you will be able to go through them with the comfort of our Lord.

In this world, we suffer in every possible way, with or without Christ. If you are not in Christ, you suffer, and if you are in Christ, you also suffer; however, in Christ, you do not suffer alone. God is with you through all suffering. It is a beautiful promise that God has given us in Psalm 91:14–16: "Because he loves me, says the Lord I will rescue him; I will protect him, for he acknowledges my name. He will call on me, and I will answer him; I will be with him in trouble, I will deliver him and honor him. With long life I will satisfy him and show him my salvation."

The Lord will be with me in the midst of my trouble! God has not said we will not suffer, but He has promised that He will be with us until the end of time. In the same way that the afflictions of Christ are abundant in our lives, Christ Himself is our consolation. He will not give anyone more than they can handle. Therefore, when a trial comes to your life, a big problem or a very difficult time—maybe your dad dies, your mom or child dies, or anyone you love—do not worry. Immediately remember that He does not give you more than you can handle. This is the first test. If God has allowed it, it is because He knows that I can handle it. It's because God has seen in me that I can survive it. If I can't handle it, it is because I am not able to believe, or I want to stop because of the trial. But it is not for any other reason.

If God has allowed it, it is because He has seen in me a capacity to move on. Listen, brothers, to what God is saying to the church. Are you listening? If we are going through trials, it is so that we can be comforted. We are comforted for your salvation and consolation. The Bible reads "If we are distressed, it is for your comfort and salvation, if we are comforted, it is for your comfort, which produces in you patient endurance of the same sufferings we suffer" (II Corinthians 1:6). When we are in the midst of suffering the same afflictions that others are going through, and our hope for you is steadfast. This is how we know that we are together in our afflictions and in our consolation.

Just like God has comforted us, I believe that our comfort will reach many. We do not doubt that the consolation my wife and I have received has been a comfort to others. God came to comfort us. Was His Word fulfilled? Yes, because we were comforted for your consolation. I know that if on that day, I would have allowed myself to cry without being comforted, many of you would have gone home heartbroken. But that day, God gave me the strength and also gave it to you. As the comfort of God descended upon me, it was also reaching many of you. If we have been comforted, it is so that we can comfort others. That is very clear in the Word. God has said it. I hope that you do not forget this. When you face trials, ask God for His comfort so that you can be of help to others. God comforts your life, and you will be able to comfort others. We hope that the fruits of the death of David Daniel will be beautiful. Blessed are those who die in the Lord.

Frances and I are very happy, and I want you to be aware of this. We have our confidence in God. Yes, beloved, God has comforted us in a beautiful way, and we strive forward, trusting in Him. We are so happy to have such a beautiful Christ. We feel honored and blessed in having the faith and hope that Jesus Christ has given us. We know that all things work together for the good of those who love Him. Frances and I have been able to comfort some of you with the comfort that Christ has given us".

Our congregation received comfort through Danny's message that day.

Parents who mourned the death of a child have been comforted when we shared the testimony of how God comforted us in the death of David. When Danny was in Riobamba, Ecuador, teaching at a retreat, there were seventeen couples of Quechua indigenous pastors. Danny shared with them the death of David and how God comforted us. At the end, a pastor came up and asked for prayer because his daughter had just died. No one had come to comfort him, and he felt very alone. Immediately, Danny hugged him and prayed for him. We glorify God because this pastor, who was the chief of the Indians, received consolation at this time.

We can never forget David Daniel, his birthday or the day of his departure. God has comforted us. David Daniel was our beloved son, and we will love him forever. I wrote a goodbye poem to David Daniel that I want to share with you:

> David Daniel
>
> Goodbye, my dear son.
> I will see you soon.
> We will see each other one day.
> Wait for me. Rest with my Lord.
> You will not suffer. You will sleep,
>
> Yes, you will sleep in the arms of the angels,
> While you wait for your parents.
> If you talk to Jesus, my dear son,
> Whisper in His ear,
> that I will always love you.

There are many who have asked, "Does the death of a younger child hurt more than the death of an older loved one?" I have not lost a grown child, but I know that the pain a mother's heart feels is deep, no matter the age. David Daniel was a son who was loved deeply since the first day he was place in my womb, and it hurt me a lot to see my little one die.

I think that when we have a child for longer periods of time, there are more memories, and the experience of losing that child may be more painful. I believe with all my heart that God can comfort those who are mourning because He did it with me and His promise is eternal life. It encourages us to believe and wait for the resurrection of the dead. That promise is for all who have received Christ as their Savior. If our loved ones have believed and received Christ in their hearts, they will be resurrected when Christ returns (1 Corinthians 15:52 and Thessalonians 4:16).

Several years after our son David's death, Danny's half-brother, Juan, died of leukemia in Puerto Rico. Danny was with his mom, and that night, he told her about God's consolation and said to her, "Mom, I know the pain you are going through because my son died, and I want to tell you that the God that comforted me is here to comfort you." From that moment on, his mom stopped crying and was comforted.

On November 1, 2006, death knocked again at the door of our family. In Louisville, Kentucky, our dear grandson Tyler Enrique McQueary went to be with the Lord. We went to Louisville to comfort our children Frances and Brian. God has given Tyler's twin brother, Breyton Rey, loving parents and two other brothers, Alex and Cameron. Breyton is a healthy and beautiful boy. God has comforted our children.

Dear reader, Christ came to comfort those who are mourning in their hearts.[7] If you are mourning in this moment and you are sad, believe in God and ask Him to comfort you. Believe in His promises of eternal life. Let the Word of God penetrate your heart and comfort you. Lord, God of all consolation, I ask that you wipe

---

7   Isaiah 61:2

away every tear of each brother and sister in mourning at this hour and that they receive comfort. Amen!

One Step from Death

Twice in his life, Danny has been on the verge of death, but it was not the time to go home. Those were tough times, shocking and never forgotten. At the same time, these moments motivated us to meditate and reflect on life.

The first time happened eleven years ago. Danny and I were returning on a bus from Comayagua with a group of American volunteers. We left the group in a camp and drove to San Pedro Sula. A few minutes later, the bus was hit by a pickup truck. Danny was sitting in the front, and his body flew through the windshield and landed on the roof of the pickup truck.

At first, Danny thought he was dead, but soon he began to hear voices and realized he was alive. Danny couldn't feel his hands because he had broken his fingers. He got down and saw that the passenger of the truck was dead and the driver was badly wounded. While he was walking toward the bus, he was surprised when a neighbor who lived across the road stared at him and said, "Raise your hands and worship the Lord." Danny raised his hands and worshipped God.

I was inside the bus when Danny came over and asked me if I was okay. I told him, "I believe my leg and some ribs are broken." He tried to stop the cars passing by us to get help, but nobody stopped. But God saw him from heaven and sent a group of young believers in our direction. A young man recognized Danny in the middle of the road and said, "Stop! That's the pastor who was preaching in our church last week."

Immediately they took us to a hospital in San Pedro Sula. During the journey to the hospital, we worshipped and praised God for His mercies. My heart was filled with joy, knowing that God preserved our lives and that I would be able to see my children again.

The crash had broken three of my ribs and my left leg's femur. I needed surgery immediately. At the hospital, the doctor asked me, "Who are you?" I said, "My husband is a pastor, and I am a teacher. Why?"

"I received a call from the United States stating that an air ambulance was on the way to pick you up. The ambulance service will cost more than fifteen thousand dollars. Now I know you have somebody up there," he said while he was pointing to the sky.

That night, someone had called our friend and brother in Christ, Dr. Laurence Arnold. Immediately, he made the necessary arrangements and paid for the plane to move us to a Florida hospital. God used him to bless us. We will always be grateful to Dr. Arnold.

We give glory to God, who has never left us in the midst of the tribulation. Praise God that Liza, who was not hurt, had moved from my side to the back of the bus a few minutes before the accident. Liza was able to take care of both Danny and I. She was our sweet nurse for four months. It was not easy. I could not walk, and Danny could not use his hands; however, God gave us His strength and the best nurse.

My brave husband returned to Honduras four days after surgery with Dr. Arnold and his medical team. His medical condition did not prevent him from going to bless many Hondurans with medical services and preach the Word of God.

When I arrived home from the hospital, it was raining. That night, the roof of our house was leaking next to my bed. God was looking down. That same week, He touched members from the First Baptist Church of Pompano Beach and Calvary Chapel Church of Fort Lauderdale to build us a new roof. For two weeks, families from the Spanish Mission of Soncoast Church in Boca Raton brought us food. At my school, the staff and children collected money and food. For the following weeks, we received various groups of ladies from different churches who came to clean and cook.

Through the time of this tribulation, God's provision flooded our house so abundantly that we were able to share our blessings with other needy families. We had dedicated our lives to serving and giving since we had been teenagers. This time, we had to sit still and receive.

On the Sunday before the accident, Danny went to San Pedro Sula's airport, where he met a brother in Christ from Louisiana. His wife had died while she was diving in the islands of Honduras. Danny shared some words of encouragement and prayed for him. When we came back from the hospital, God surprised us. We opened the mail, and there was a letter from this brother in Christ from Louisiana saying, "Pastor Danny, it seems that your ministry was in the heart of this family. They requested that in lieu of flowers, we give donations to your ministry. I enclose a check with this note." When we looked at the date of the letter, it was written three days before our accident. God was watching over us before, during, and after the accident.

The second time Danny was close to death happened in 2008. The day before he was set to leave for Argentina, Danny had appendicitis. Three days after the surgery, he was swollen, and his condition worsened. Danny said, "Frances, I feel very sick. If God calls me home, I do not want you or our children to be angry with Him. Do not blame God because if He calls me, I will go. I had a good life dedicated to serving the Lord."

I hugged him and said tearfully, "No, you will not die. Maybe at this moment you feel like you are in the valley of death, but fear not. You will live." I was praying for him until he fell asleep. That afternoon, he went through surgery again because his intestines had collapsed. I called our children, who came to be with their dad. He spent fifteen days in the hospital. Our God sustained Danny and saved his life instead of allowing him to take the nine-hour flight to Argentina. I strongly believe that Danny still has a long way to go.

Chapter 6: *Avance Misionero's Plan in Honduras*

In 1972, we went to Puerto Rico for a short time when our daughter Rebecca was born, and five months later, we returned to Honduras. We now had a vision and plan for the work the Lord had directed Danny to accomplish. The Lord had told Danny that he needed to return to Honduras to direct the missionary work so that he would not forget that he had been called to be a shepherd.

Danny's passion for the lost souls was more intense, and his heart beat with more force and desire to work for the Lord and to do what he had been entrusted to do. He gathered the missionaries Judith Santiago, Gabriel Álvarez, Rubén Nieves, and Felícita Pérez and began praying and studying the Word of God.

During that time in Honduras, the evangelists (they called anyone who was Protestant an evangelist) were not welcomed in Comayagua because the neighborhood was predominantly traditional Catholic. At night, we could hear the sound of stones on the roof while we prayed and worshipped in song. Several years later, I learned that Danny had hidden an anonymous threat telling us to leave the city or be killed. Nothing made this servant of the Lord desist from doing what he knew the Lord wanted him to do. He ignored the threats, and with courage, he continued to work with the missionaries in our house for six months without telling anyone about the threats.

One night when we were singing songs of praise, we heard a knock on the door. It was a soldier who had heard the singing and had decided to come to the house. His name was Lázaro Morales. He was a *garífuna*[8] native from Trujillo, a region in northern Honduras. He lived in front of our house in Comayagua. He belonged to the Fifth Battalion. We opened the door and greeted him and then told him to come the next day. Lázaro stated that he could not return the next day because this was his only day off.

Danny allowed him to stay for the Bible study. We had no idea that the Lord had a special plan for his life. He was attentive to the Bible teachings and remained quiet when the missionaries brought a container with water to begin a feet-washing ceremony. One of the missionaries asked Danny, "Why don't we invite the young man to come so we can wash his feet?"

Danny was surprised by the request. He thought he was a visitor, but he agreed. The missionaries came to the soldier and asked him if he would allow them to wash his feet, and he graciously accepted. Right away, they took his boots off and lovingly washed his feet. When they finished, the same missionary asked, "Danny, why don't we invite him to accept Christ as his personal savior?"

Danny asked Lázaro if we would like to accept Christ as his personal savior, and the man did! This was his day of salvation!

---

8   A mixture of Arawak, Caribbean Islands, and African slaves.

Truly, the Lord has His timing! Who would have thought that during a feet-washing ceremony someone would receive God's salvation?

This young man was the first person who received Christ as his personal savior through the ministering of the Avance Misionero in Honduras, and once he finished his military duty, he stayed with the missionaries to learn how to be a minister. Today, Lázaro is the pastor of the Santa Fe community in the city of Trujillo.[9] It is amazing that Lázaro returned to his people to preach and teach the Word of God. Praise the Lord!

The Lord provided Danny and the other missionaries with the strategies to win the city of Comayagua for Christ. We began to visit each home in groups of two. We made friends who little by little started to come and listen to the small church services we had in the carport. The neighborhood became curious, and many began to ask, "Who are these young people who speak so beautifully about Christ?"

Each day, the Lord was adding those who were going to receive the blessing of salvation. For example, young Orlando Sierra and his relatives joined the group. Then Mariela Campos invited her friend Lolita Magaña, who brought Gloria, Melba, Aracelis, and others. Little by little, a spiritual family began to grow in the love of the Lord and began attending the Bible studies we held in the carport of the house.

Jaime Vallecillo and his father, José Eulogio Vallecillo, known as Cuyuyo, came to the Bible studies thirsty for the Word of God. Cuyuyo came to the Bible studies without shoes. He walked

---

9   county in northern Honduras

barefooted throughout the city, and sometimes he would say to me, "Sister Frances, can I help you set the chairs and clean the carport, where we have our Bible studies?" Every Saturday with a smile full of love, Cuyuyo would take the broom from my hand and eagerly sweep and clean the place of worship. I can't forget that he changed my name and called me "*Sor* Frances."

Cuyuyo became part of the history of Avance Misionero's work in Honduras. Once the Central de Comayagua Church tabernacle was built, this servant of the Lord dedicated over twenty years of his life to keep and clean the temple. He slept in the church, cleaned the sanctuary, and joyfully opened the doors for the services so that God's people could enter to worship Him.

Those who came to visit the church would take home the picture of his joyful servant, who welcomed them and shared his love for the house of worship. Danny and I love, admire, and acknowledge the beautiful work this servant did in the house of the Lord. On October 2008, our beloved Cuyuyo went home with the Lord at the ripe age of ninety-five. He left us a legacy of dedication, service, and love for others.

The group continued to grow, and it had its first retreat in the neighborhood of Jamalteca, a community close to the city of Libertad. There was a natural waterfall in the *hacienda* where the first members of the Avance Misionero en Honduras Church were baptized.

One time, we went to minister with another church, and the missionaries we left behind conducted the Bible study. When we returned, we were surprised to see them still there. Some of them had been baptized with the Holy Spirit and other were speaking in other tongues and prophesying. They were all worshipping and praising God. This is how the Avance Misionero Church revival started.

Before long, I began a children's Bible study in Comayagua with seven children, and a year and a half later, we had four children's studies and a youth group. By that time, other missionaries had arrived from Puerto Rico. Lucy Nieves, Ramón Nieves, and Ana M. Hernández became involved with the children and youth ministry.

Later on, Gladys Pérez, Nelly Westerband, and Milagros Chervoni, who were also from Puerto Rico, were added to the missionary group. It was wonderful to see how each one of them was fulfilling the call according to God's plan. They preached, ministered to the children, visited the brethren, and helped with anything that we asked of them.

Sister Judith Santiago organized and led the first Bible Institute of the Avance Misionero in Honduras. With the help of other missionaries, she was able to teach and prepare workers that would become the future preachers in Honduras. Today, Avance Misionero is staffed with these pastors.

Danny began his first radio program called *Variedades Cristianas* with emotion and excitement. The program had a short section for in-depth Bible study called "Searching the Scriptures." This is how people heard the voice of the humble preacher over the radio waves in the nearby neighborhoods around the city of Comayagua every Sunday at 11:00 a.m.

Soon we had opportunities to plant new churches in some of the mountain villages. Therefore, the missionaries Gabriel Álvarez and Ramón Nieves were sent to preach by our church in Puerto

Rico. A few months later, they planted the first church at a village named Lajas.

Anita Hernández and Ramón Nieves planted a church in the neighborhood called the *Independencia*, a suburb of Comayagua. Lucy Nieves helped them with the evangelism program, and the church began to grow quickly.

In January 1976, Danny rented a place downtown called the Real Caxa, which is an open air field surrounded by ruins of buildings that had been built by the Spaniards. There, he held the first evangelistic crusade in Comayagua. Many souls received Christ, including Teresa Cáceres, Fanny Suazo, and along with some of their relatives. He held a Bible study in their neighborhood every week to teach them the Word of God.

The missionaries planted churches in different cities. One of the first ones was in the city of La Paz. For many years, the church held the services at the Zacapa's family home, where the Holy Spirit touched so many lives. The church grew, and some young adults were called to study at the Bible Institute in Comayagua.

Nehemías, Manuel, Reina, and Edelmira left their homes to live in Comayagua and study. They were so excited. They studied hard, graduated, and started serving the Lord. Today, Edelmira and Manuel are serving at a local church in La Paz. Reina is a missionary in Jinotega, Nicaragua. Nehemías Chavarría was the Avance Misionero's director for many years. He planted two churches in San Pedro Sula, and he is the pastor of one of the churches and the director of the Bible Institute.

The missionaries taught the Word on a weekly basis at the homes and planted churches in Danlí, San Pedro Sula, and Tegucigalpa.

God's plan for those missionaries was awesome. In about three years of work, they were able to establish missions in different provinces of Honduras, the Bible Institute in Comayagua, and the Ebenezer Elementary School. The seed of God's Word was planted, germinated and bore fruit. Praise God!

I am a witness of the love that Danny and these missionaries had for the unbelievers. They left everything in Puerto Rico and sacrificed to fulfill its mission. Under heavy rain, sometimes without food, they ran with a small umbrella up to homes where they would teach Bible study. Their motto was this: "We have to be responsible and fulfill our mission." And they did it. They worked hard, sowing in tears and making sacrifices. They fasted, prayed, studied the Word deeply, and then went out to preach. I know my husband and those brave and dedicated missionaries one day will receive a reward from their Lord. Amen. "His master replied, 'Well done, good and faithful servant! You have been faithful with a few things; I will put you in charge of many things. Come and share your master's happiness!' (Matthew 25:21)

The Lord granted me the authority to stay in charge of education, so I kept working on the Bible school each week, believing that this was my only mission in Honduras. I was wrong. God had other plans for me. The following year, the Lord told me, "Frances, establish a primary school." Danny and I believed God and began planning.

Professor Adam Suazo and his beloved wife Berta Zacapa Suazo guided and helped us through the process. We had no money, property, furniture, or students. We just had two teachers Anita Hernández and myself, but we had the greatest thing a person can have—faith in God.

We presented the application to the Ministry of Education in Tegucigalpa[10] to obtain official approval to open the school in February 1975. The staff there asked us for a list of the enrolled students, but we did not have one. With a notebook in hand, Anita and I walked the streets of San Sebastián, Comayagua, seeking the names of prospective students for the future private school Ebenezer.

Without knowing us, the parents opened the doors of their homes and enrolled their children, which allowed us to begin the development of God's plan with the school. We arrived at the mission house late at night, fatigued and tired but happy with the full enrollment for kindergarten and first grade. During the following weeks, we continued the appropriate arrangements.

With great joy, on February 17, 1975, Ebenezer School opened in the neighborhood of San Sebastián in Comayagua. It was a labor of love. God used Mr. and Mrs. Suazo, Mr. Carlos Yuja, his beloved wife, Elena Vindel, who was our first pro bono director, the teachers Mirna Vindel, Thelma Vindel, Teresa Cáceres, Elsa Lagos, and other friends who guided and supported us in the school project.

I cannot forget the kindness and generosity of people like Mrs. Adriana Rodríguez, who lent us a house of two rooms in front of the San Sebastián church, which we managed and molded into our little school. Mr. Quintín Polanco donated the wood to make furniture. Mr. Julio Lagos was the carpenter who made and painted the chairs and tables for students with the help of missionaries and some fellow church members. Some church ladies, friends,

---

10   Honduras city capital

and missionaries helped to make flower arrangements and crafts, which we sold to buy books, supplies, and educational materials.

God sent us the teacher and missionary Gladys Pérez, who joined to teach pro bono for many years in the school. Our greatest reward was seeing the first class of sixth grade at the school. I have no words to thank these servants of the Lord and to acknowledge their love, sacrifice, and dedication. For a few months, we also had the blessing of two volunteer teachers from Puerto Rico, Gilda Díaz and María I. Rivera (Chela).

How can we thank Lázaro Morales for helping in the school? While this young man was studying at the Bible Institute at night, he took care of the school, ran errands, and played with children without receiving a salary.

In the most difficult time at the school, Danny, along with pastors Orlando Sierra, Nehemías Chavarría, and Avance Misionero congregations in Honduras, fought to keep the doors open when local authorities wanted to close the institution down. The teaching positions that the government paid were reallocated to another campus. With fewer teachers, it was necessary to get money to pay salaries for new teachers. When he returned to Florida, Danny shared the school's needs, and many generous hearts began to work together to pay the teachers. God gave us the victory, and the school was not closed.

Currently, the school has an excellent staff and administration. Ms. Delfina Sierra is the director. It has an enrollment of more than 250 students. In addition to an academic education, students receive daily Bible lessons. During these years, the work of each member of staff and management has not been in vain. Many students and families have been reached with the gospel and serve the Lord today.

In Piedras Bonitas, on the lot donated by Mr. and Mrs. Carlos Yuja, Ebenezer School has been like a beacon from its high location, one that shines with the instruction and the gospel to the city of Comayagua. Today, many alumni work as doctors, engineers, pilots, secretaries, teachers, pastors and other good occupations designed to serve their communities.

God gave us the name "Ebenezer", which means, "... Thus far, the Lord has helped us. 1~Samuel 7:12". Ebenezer would be the motto of the school because the school was God's instrument to help children and introduce them to Christ. I can say that the school's mission has been fulfilled, thanks to the Lord and each person who has helped.

Chapter 7: 1980 Honduras' Year

In 1980, God told us, "This is the year of Honduras." We did not understand that phrase until we realized that we needed to construct a building for the school. Danny began to make the plans to build. We were encouraged to pray, and we believed that if God had told us this course of action, we would be able to accomplish it.

For five years, the teachers and students had been roaming around like nomads from one neighborhood to another throughout Comayagua, renting houses to hold our classes. Building a school was a beautiful project, but even though we had the orders to begin construction, we only had forty dollars in the account.

God was already touching hearts in Puerto Rico to build the school. A few weeks later, we had the arrival of Eduvigis Rivera, Domingo Gonzalez, Brother Moisés Avilés, and his wife, Lolita (parents of the deceased missionary Moisés Aviles). The members of Avance Misionero worked very hard with these servants of the Lord, and in four months, we finished building the school on the land that Mr. and Mrs. Carlos Yuja had generously donated.

The school is located on a hill in the Piedras Bonitas neighborhood in Comayagua. Three large classrooms were built, and they were divided so that all six grades could be held and we could work out of a small office. With great joy, we inaugurated the school, with the presence of the distinguished First Lady of Honduras, Professor Aida de Suazo Córdova, the school superintendent Leonardo Lagos, and many other distinguished guests.

Mission accomplished. The school was built, and we still had the forty dollars in the bank because God had provided everything—money, materials, land, and workers to build the school.

That same year, we had to build a sanctuary for the congregation in the city of Comayagua. With the forty dollars in the bank, Danny began making the plans to build the sanctuary. Danny wanted to be obedient and do what God had told him to do. When he saw a vacant lot at the entrance of the city, he went and investigated who the owner of the land was because he wanted to help God with His plan.

He went and spoke to the owner, Dr. Pereira, and asked him if he would rent the land to us for three years to keep a mobile wooden tabernacle there. God's good helper thought, *In three years, if we have to move to another lot, we can just move the tabernacle.*

After he heard Danny's request, the doctor said he would talk it over with his family and let him know what the answer was at a later time. A few weeks later, the doctor called Danny and told him, "Pastor, my family and I want to give you the land for you to build your church."

Danny asked every member of the church to bring small smooth rocks so that they could write their name on each. Each member, including the children, brought a rock with their name written on them. Then they placed these rocks on the land where they would soon build the temple. There by faith, the congregation and Danny proclaimed that a sanctuary would be built within that year, and it was so. The tabernacle was completed that year.

Frances Morales

Chapter 8: Helping God

While Danny was in Siguatepeque, he came up with the great idea to set up a chicken farm. He started thinking, *after I sell all my chicken, I will be able to support myself in Honduras.*

He began to research the details so that he could start his new adventure as a chicken farmer. Danny was so excited as he made proceeds from his farm. Little did he know then, however, that God had others plans for him. He hadn't called Danny to be a chicken farmer. After a while, Danny understood that the Lord wanted him to live by faith, trusting Him!

One day, he became very ill with a serious case of hepatitis. His eyes turned yellow, and the high fever kept him in bed for many days. The doctor said to Danny, "Young man, I recommend you pack your stuff, leave this country, and return home if you don't want to die here. You are very sick."

Very weak, he went back home with those words banging in his mind: "Go back home … you may die here." The same day, a missionary from the United States named Brother Benjamin La Font visited Danny. He prayed for Danny's healing, and before he left, he got a $10.00 bill and said, "The Lord told me to give you this offering. It has a message for you." The missionary left, and Danny understood the message from God immediately: "I will take care of your needs. Trust Me."

The following day, Danny felt better and took a walk downtown, where he saw the doctor, who was amazed to see Danny walking around. He asked, "What are you doing here?" "God healed me," Danny answered and kept walking praising the Lord. "And the prayer offered in faith will make the sick person well; the Lord will raise them up. If they have sinned, they will be forgiven" (James 5:15).

Other times, Danny received ideas and proposals that would allow him to start small businesses and make a good income. He even tried to keep a Christian bookstore in Comayagua, but it didn't work. He was offered housing, churches, a car, and a salary. They were very good offers, but he understood that those were not included in God's plan for his life. He said no to many of the opportunities he had to be a pastor in Puerto Rico and Honduras with some ministries, but he decided to do what he was called to do in Honduras.

In 1984, we moved to Florida. Again, Danny had to make similar decisions. He prayed and asked the Lord, "Are these for me?" The answer was no. Danny continued to live by faith and trust the Lord, who called him.

Danny had been living His promise: "My God will provide all things according to His richest" (Philippians 4:19).

Chapter 9: Living by Faith

Jehovah Jireh: God Is My Provider!

During these forty years in ministry, God has made provision for all the needs of His servant, Danny, his family, and the missionaries. At this time, I wish to share some experiences where God's care and provision has been manifested.

With the love offerings from the Bible classes in Puerto Rico, we would buy the groceries for the Missionary House and ourselves. Each missionary received twenty-two American dollars, an equivalent of forty-four lempiras (Honduran currency), according to the monetary exchange rate at that time. Two weeks passed without receiving our correspondence and love offerings from Puerto Rico. One afternoon, with sadness, I told the missionary girls, "We have no food. There is one egg that I will cook for our daughter, Rebecca, and half a bag of beans." Rebecca was barely a year old, and I was pregnant with Frances. The girls told me, "No problem Frances. We will fast."

Soon after, somebody knocked at the door. It was a nurse named Sister María de la Paz Ortiz (Mariela). She was attending Bible studies and told me she wanted to speak to me in private. We went to the bedroom because I thought she was going to talk to me about something that was troubling her. She said, "I want to invite you to dinner tonight." Thrilled, I asked her; "What time do you want Danny and I to arrive?"

She responded, "Sister Frances, I made food for everyone and wanted permission to bring the food here because you have a big table." I was wrong. The blessing was for all of us. I didn't know God had a special catering service for us. The meal was delicious. The missionaries looked at each other as we ate and kept our situation to ourselves. Years later, we shared with the sister the testimony of how the Lord had used her that day, providing such a delicious and abundant meal that lasted for two days.

Then a secretary at the Santa Teresa Hospital heard the voice of the Lord telling her to go to the market and buy groceries for the missionaries. She was Lolita Magaña, a young woman who was beginning to attend Bible studies. She never went to the market, but she obeyed the Lord and went shopping for us. Overcoming her shyness, she entered the house with the groceries, not knowing that God had used her as an instrument to bless us during this time of scarcity.

A Deer, a Shotgun ... a Provision from God!

Another day, some friends from town invited Danny to go hunting with them. He was very excited when he left and later returned home in a pickup truck. We all went outside when we heard someone blowing the horn and people yelling. The returning hunters were branding a dead deer on the hood of the pickup truck. They were yelling; "Danny killed it," and they went on to display it up and down the streets. It was the news headline of the day. With an old shotgun and one shell, Danny had made the shot that had brought about the blessing. We ate deer meat for two weeks. We cooked it as steaks and stew. It was delicious. God has angelic hunters! He sent them to help Danny. God provided food until the regular offering from Puerto Rico arrived.

Out of Milk and Out of Money

On the morning of April 5, 1978, we left the clinic with our beautiful new offspring, Daniel Isaías. We were very happy with our precious baby boy. But in a second, our happiness would be transformed in sadness and uncertainty. With only two lempiras to pay for a taxi fare, the little can of powdered milk we had for the baby fell to the ground and spilled when we were descending the few steps of the clinic. Danny picked it up as fast as he could, and to my surprise, there was little milk left in the can. The measuring spoon rolled down the ground too, and in desperation, Danny picked it up and put it inside the can. "Danny, you just contaminated the milk," I said, almost crying. I was heartbroken because I was not able to breastfeed my child and we did not have money to get more milk. We got in the taxi and went home very sad. Danny told me, "I will find someone to sell me milk on credit."

I asked God to not let my baby cry. He was asleep when my good friend Mrs. Nena Yuja arrived. She saw the baby, and after we had chatted for a long time, she told me that she had not bought a present because she and her husband wanted to give us a hundred lempiras (equivalent to fifty dollars) to buy something for the child. When she gave me the money, I began to cry.

I called Danny and showed him the money, knowing that it was God's answer to our problem with the milk for little Danny. We thanked God and shared with Mrs. Yuja how God was using her at that very moment to bless us because we did not have money to buy milk for the baby. For the month that followed, offerings and gifts continued to arrive. God provided what was needed for our child.

God Answered My Prayer

One day, our doctor told me that we needed to circumcise our son immediately before he was a month old. I had no money, and I was alone. Danny was at the capital, training for radio broadcasting. I called him and explained what the doctor had told me, and he said that we did not have much money. I reminded him that his mom had sent some, and he told me to go ahead and travel with the boy to Tegucigalpa. I found a ride to Tegucigalpa the following day.

That night, I lay prostrate before the Lord and asked Him to repay my husband all the money we would spend on the operation. The following day, doctors operated on little Danny, and in the afternoon, we returned to Comayagua. We had spent one hundred lempiras (fifty dollars).

When we arrived home, one of the missionaries handed Danny an envelope containing one hundred lempiras without a note or message. We only had the name of the person who had left it. Danny began to wonder what that money was for and wanted to call the person. I told him that I did not know what it was for but that I had prayed to the Lord the night before and had asked that all the money we had spent be returned to us. I could not convince him, and he called the sister who had sent the money, Raquel Reyes from San Pedro Sula.

She shared the testimony that the morning before, she heard the voice of God telling her on two occasions to bring an offering to His servant Danny in Comayagua. She dismissed the voice and went about her daily chores. She went to visit "Granny," an anointed and consecrated servant from the Central Reformed Church of San Pedro Sula. There, "Granny" confirmed that she had been called to give an offering to Danny. When she traveled to Tegucigalpa, she stopped in Comayagua and dropped off her offering. Thus, Danny received confirmation that God had once again provided for our needs.

One Chicken and Twenty-Two Guests!

One evening before I started preparing dinner, a Nicaraguan refugee family fleeing the conflict between the Sandinistas and Contras arrived at our home. All I had was one chicken, and counting all the people we had to feed, including my family, the total came to twenty-two. I decided to make chicken and rice, and I cut the chicken in pieces about an inch long. We all enjoyed an abundant and delicious dinner.

The Lord's First Fruits

I remember Sister Socorro Quan, a faithful Chinese descendant woman from Comayagua. She would send all the firstfruits from her farm to the church—mangos, avocados, and other fruits. Firstfruits also arrived from Brother Ismael Ortiz in the form of bales of corn. We would marvel at the quantity of food and the size of the fruits they brought to the house of the Lord. God blessed the work of their hands.

Horchata for the Offering

For many years, Sister Coca made the best *horchata* (a sweet drink made of rice and spices) sold in the market of Comayagua. Month after month, the sister would bring her horchata offering to the Lord. It was like the Old Testament widow's oil jar. Every month the horchata sale would be more profitable. With that offering, a lot of ministry expenses were covered, and many of the brethren in need were assisted.

Wrapped with love and care

Danny was somewhat worried because as a result of the bad economic times in the United States of America, many of our sponsors had to stop sending their regular monthly support to the Cántaros de Bendición ministry. One afternoon, Danny received a call from Brother Robert Lloyd, who collaborated with the ministry for many years. After they exchanged greetings, Brother Lloyd said, "Danny, I want to come by to drop off three avocados." He arrived home with the three best-looking avocados in the state of Florida, three avocados wrapped with the love and care that were characteristic of Robert and his wife, Ann.

While they were talking, Robert said, "Danny, in addition to these avocados, I brought you an offering for your ministry." Once again, the provision was delivered into the hands of God's servant.

Love Offerings

There have been many people in Puerto Rico, Honduras, United States, and other countries who have approached Danny with monetary offerings. With God's love reflected on their faces, they have said, "Brother Danny, God put in my heart to give you this offering." The Lord's provision never failed. Blessed be His name!

Frances Morales

Chapter 10: Enlarge the Place of Your Tent

This phrase is widely used among the people of God when one is talking about extending the work of evangelism. In the fall of 1983, God told Danny to leave Honduras and move to Pompano, Florida. The prophecy that God had given him many years ago while he was in Puerto Rico came to his mind now: "Danny, you will go to many states." It is sometimes difficult to understand God's timing when you are doing His work. More than ten years had passed, and no doors had opened to go to the States. I had seen in Danny a servant waiting for God's time to move, recognizing the voice of God and believing God.

At that time, the work in Honduras was established, bearing beautiful fruit. However, Danny did not ask God, "Why now?" Obediently, he began to put everything in place for the family trip and mission. He had a group of Honduran workers willing to give everything to continue the work of Avance Misionero in Honduras. He organized all the work, placing the workers in their respective ministries, schools, Bible Institute, and established churches.

Between hugs and tears, we said goodbye to our beloved Honduran brothers and sisters. We left January 9, 1984, for the state of Florida to enlarge the place of our tent. We stayed with my loving aunt Carmen Touchette for two months. Then we moved to a beautiful house in Pompano Beach on March 26, which we were able to buy thanks to the kindness of Mr. and Mrs. Carlos Yuja, who lent us the money for the down payment.

Those first months were very difficult. We practiced the English we had learned in Puerto Rico. It was not easy to make friends and find a job. God's faithfulness was demonstrated once again by providing us with jobs, and the children began to learn English too. Danny's first occupation was a cleaning job in a maintenance company. Doing this humble job did not make him feel bad because by doing it, he could support his family. It was a pleasure to see him come home happy with money for expenses. He later got a job at Scotty's Hardware Store, where little by little, he learned hardware vocabulary with the help of Mike, his supervisor, who also helped him understand the customers. Danny shared his rice and beans every day at lunch as a way of thanking his boss.

It was a big change for a pastor. After he had been in a pulpit surrounded by the love of his flock, he was now in another country, cleaning bathrooms and loading building materials. It was not an easy task. Danny was a pastor, not a company worker. Was God wrong? No way. The Lord had a plan for Danny in this country. Working to support his family, he learned to communicate with Anglo-Americans. This was necessary for his future ministry in the United States.

In 1986, they closed Scotty's Hardware Store, and Danny lost his job. I was working at Worden's World of Crafts in Pompano Beach. My co-worker, Priscilla, asked the manager, Steve Worden, "Do you have a job here for Frances's husband? He has no job and has four children to feed." Steve asked me, "What does your husband do?" And I said, "He preaches. Well ... at home, he does everything."

The next day, Mr. Steven Worden interviewed Danny and gave him a job. In the store, he did everything, but in his toolbox, he always had a Bible to read at lunch. Steve, the manager, invited his employees to a time of prayer every Monday at 7:00 a.m., and he asked Danny to share the Word of God and to lift to God the employees' prayer requests. In this way, Danny, speaking little English at that time, began his ministry in the lounge of a craft shop in the state of Florida.

Months later, the Worden family became interested in the work of this missionary, which barely knew English but would not stop talking about God and the mission field. We all planned the first trip to Honduras and raised funds to help the pastors in Honduras that Danny had mentored.

Working with Youth for Christ

Through Mr. Truman Worden, Danny met Rick Englert, who worked with Youth for Christ. Danny got involved in this organization and began to lead groups of volunteers to Honduras. These groups built an orphanage, several churches, and a one-room annex for Ebenezer School. With this organization, Danny also had the opportunity to visit England, Kenya, and Brazil and establish the ministry of Youth for Christ in Honduras.

A New Ministry
Cántaros de Bendición (Pitchers of Blessings)

A few years later, Danny decided to start his own ministry in Florida, which he called Cántaros de Bendición. The mission of this ministry has been to evangelize, restore lives, and help those in need here and abroad. It has a board of directors and many supporters. Doors were opened to preach in churches, youth retreats, weddings, and conferences in Florida, several other states, and Hispanic countries.

During this time, Danny began to preach and teach the Word in English and Spanish. I remember he delivered his first sermon in English in Winchester, Virginia. His preaching was very short, barely ten minutes. I was shivering, but it was not cold. At the end of the service, Danny saw that the brothers began to remove the pews and told the pastor, "Sorry, I didn't want to destroy this church!" Amid the laughter of those present, he learned that they were going to renovate the church.

On another occasion when we went to North Carolina, he told the congregation with his characteristic humor, "I brought glue to paste the pieces of my broken English and correction fluid to erase any bad words I say." So, he got the attention of the congregation and preached for about fifteen minutes. Gradually, he acquired more vocabulary and fluency with the language, and eventually, he lost the fear of preaching in English.

A Pulpit for Thirteen Million

It seems incredible, but now Danny teaches the Word of God weekly to thirteen million listeners in the Caribbean as well as

Central and South America through CVC LA VOZ Christian radio station based in Miami. This station has given Danny the opportunity to preach through a free radio show for eleven years. His messages have reached more than twenty countries. The program has the goal of encouraging and stimulating the pastors and church leaders.

Many pastors have written and testified about how they have been restored and encouraged by the teachings of this radio program. Some of these pastors extended invitations to Danny to go and visit their countries. Through his radio program, he has organized retreats for pastors and their wives in Honduras, Bolivia, Ecuador, Nicaragua, Paraguay, Argentina, and Chile.

Partners in Ministry

Danny has a ministry partner after God's heart. I am referring to the Reverend Carlos Armenteros, pastor of the Manantial de Vida Baptist Church in Miami. He has been a great blessing to Danny's life and ministry. He is like a Joshua to Moses who has supported the ministry for years. He has collaborated with Danny, teaching the Word on the radio, in churches, and at retreats. He and his wife, Elizabeth, have ministered at marriage conferences under Cántaros de Bendición Ministry in different countries. Both men have been instruments of God for His glory, and his congregation has supported them and the ministry through prayer, financial support, donations, and volunteer groups for many years.

The support of the ministry from other churches and pastors has been essential for the encouragement of pastors in many countries. The Community Church in Miami and its pastor, Reverend Héctor Maradiaga, have been faithful sponsors since the beginning of this ministry. Their support, prayers, donations, and volunteers have been a great blessing.

Our pastor, Jim Letizia, and the New Covenant Church of Pompano Beach have blessed the ministry with prayers and financial support, and on several occasions, he has been with us in Honduras, where he shared the Word in pastoral retreats.

The Soncoast Church in Boca Raton has supported the ministry spiritually as well as financially. With its former pastor, Chris Cowen, and willing volunteers, the church has helped to construct several projects in Honduras. The First Baptist Church of Pompano Beach and its pastor has been a mainstay in the Cántaros de Bendición Ministry with its financial and spiritual support. On one occasion, they joined us with one hundred members of the congregation on a trip to Honduras. It was truly amazing to see them learning to speak and sing in Spanish over the course of one year and to see the ladies sewing dresses for girls from the orphanage. On several occasions, this church has sent clothing and school supplies to bless the mission work in Honduras.

I do not want to overlook the beautiful group of friends and brothers from other denominations who have helped the ministry with prayer and financial support. We also have the great blessing of having the support of our children, who love the ministry and have collaborated with their offerings and translations for the Cántaros de Bendición Ministry.

Chapter 11: Leaving Footprints

A footprint is defined as a deep and profound impression or mark. Danny has left footprints on many lives during the forty years of his ministry. In this chapter, I will include some of the many testimonies from people whose lives have been touched by Danny's ministry. One of them was Pastor Sammy Johnson,[11] who wrote and dedicated the song "The Marks of a Friend" to Danny. (See Appendix 3.)

Footprints – Pastor Nehemías Chavarría

Avance Misionero Church, San Pedro Sula, Honduras

I would like to share my testimony and give thanks to God for choosing me. At the age of seventeen years old, I had a personal encounter with Jesus, and my life was changed. I was a young man without hope and future. My heart was filled with bitterness and sadness as result of a bad childhood. God changed my life using his servants, especially Brother Danny Morales. It amazed me how God brought a man from far away to Honduras to touch

---

11 [11]Sammy Johnson, youth pastor, went on a few mission trips to Honduras with Danny to lead praise and worship.

my life as His instrument. The love he gave me was unique like a father's love.

I first met him on a farm in La Paz,[12] and he asked me, "What do you want to do?"

I answered, "I want to be a pastor!"

Then he invited me to join the students at the Avance Misionero Bible Institute in Comayagua. After I prayed, I made the decision to prepare myself to be a pastor, and I went to live with the missionaries.

When I turned eighteen, Pastor Danny surprised me with a birthday party. I'd never had one before. I was embraced with the love and acceptance of my new Christian family. That meant a lot to me. I couldn't help crying like a little boy!

I am grateful to the Lord, who used His servant to lead, guide, and prepare me to fulfill God's plan for my life. I appreciate Pastor Danny for his love, guidance, and support through all these years. I want him to know how much God used him. I wonder how many people like Danny God has around this world. Maybe it is not easy to find one, but God placed one in my way. I ask God to bless him so that he may continue to be an instrument in His hands and we may imitate his faith and commitment to the Lord. I thank God for giving me a father, a pastor, a friend.

---

12   City in Central Honduras.

Footprints - Pastor Orlando Sierra

Comayagua, Honduras

I met Pastor Danny on November 1973, when my friend Lázaro Morales invited me to a Bible study. The Bible teachings led me to the Lord and strengthened my spiritual life. His faithfulness, love, and devoted service to Jesus impacted my life. For many years, I had seen how he shared the little he had with the needy. His good testimony, humbleness, and many spiritual gifts have touched and blessed my life.

His good example, love, wise advice, and prayers have encouraged me to persevere and serve God. When my twenty-one-year-old daughter, Ana Raquel, got sick with colon cancer, Brother Danny came to Honduras to pray and stay with us. When she passed away, he came with his wife to comfort us in that difficult time of sorrow. For his love and support at all times, my family and I are grateful.

He has been like a father to me, filling up the emptiness in my heart, because my daddy was killed when I was five years old. May God bless him and continue to use my brother to reach the unsaved for His glory and honor.

Footprints - Reina Pagán

Missionary in Nicaragua

I praise God for giving me the opportunity to live for many years at the home of the missionaries from Puerto Rico. The Lord used each one of them to heal my broken heart from a sad and unhappy childhood.

I grew up without a father, and the Lord used Brother Danny to be the father I didn't have. He adopted me as his own daughter, and I learned to love him as a dad. He taught me and guided me through my teenage years. The Lord used him to show me how hurt and resentful I was with a lot of people, and I was able to make the decision to forgive and be free of those feelings that had caused so much pain in my heart.

I learned to love and serve God and to live by faith, not knowing that the Lord was preparing me to be a missionary in the near future. I praise the Lord for my spiritual dad, who left footprints in my life. I will never forget what I learned while I was living at the missionary house.

Today, I am a missionary in Jinotega, Nicaragua, along with my husband, Reverend Serafín Pagán. Thanks for being God's instrument to bless me."

Footprints - Fanny M. Suazo Chavarría

San Pedro Sula, Honduras

My mother raised me in a dysfunctional family. Pastor Danny Morales led my family to the Lord. He has been like a father to me. As a young teenager, I received his guidance, advice, even a reprimand when I did something wrong. He taught me how to have a good relationship with God as my Father.

When I was under spiritual attack, the Morales family embraced me with their love and helped me to overcome and be victorious. Sometimes I wondered where I would be if I didn't have the love and help of this precious missionary family. I give thanks to the Lord for their ministry, love, and compassion for the needy. I bless the day when these servants decided to leave their island and come to Honduras to preach the gospel. The Lord will reward them in His kingdom.

Footprints - Mariela Ortiz

Avance Misionero Church in Comayagua

I met Pastor Danny in 1973, in Comayagua. I was invited to a Bible study at his home. He was God's instrument to lead me to the truth, using His Word. I changed from being a skeptical person to being a believer in Jesus. His commitment to serve God so young caught my attention, because at that time I didn't want to know anything about Christians. His loving character and willingness impacted my life.

When I was removed from my nursing position at the local hospital, Danny and the missionaries stood by me like a strong pillar, giving me the love and support I needed. God answered their prayers and I got my position back.

About twelve years ago my marriage disintegrated. Pastor Danny and his wife blessed me with their love, support and counseling during that time of crisis and pain. Now I am struggling with breast cancer, and again their love has embraced me. I was touched when Danny called Honduras when I was having surgery. I feel like I am part of his family. Recently I visited them and when I was leaving to visit my family in Georgia, Danny gave me a twenty dollar bill and said, "This is for you so you may eat something on the way." I was touched by his love and care one more time.

For the almost forty years that I have known Pastor Danny, I have seen his faithfulness, trust and communion with God. He is worthy to imitate. He always obeys God no matter what. He shared with me his desire to get more funds so he could help needy people. His loving and generous heart motivates me to be generous like him.

Footprints - Pastor Carlos Armenteros

Manantial de Vida Baptist Church, Miami

I met Danny in 1991, at the beginning of my ministry as pastor of Manantial de Vida Baptist Church in Miami. He has been the best pastoral example in my life. He is the person to whom I could always turn for godly advice. Danny has taught me to persevere serving God as a pastor and to stand firm, even in the toughest situations.

He is a faithful brother who has been with me, and my family in good times and difficult times. He touched us with his unconditional love. I have seen in Danny a genuine concern for pastors and their families when we minister together at the pastors' retreats. Danny identifies himself with their needs and laughs and cries with them. I thank God for bringing Danny into my life, to bless my family and ministry."

Footprints - Dr. Dolman Guzmán

Quito, Ecuador

Pastor Danny was invited by the Ministry Book of Life to participate in a pastors' retreat in Quito, Ecuador. I was invited to the retreat. After he shared several experiences and messages from the Word, I was touched and felt God's calling to serve Him.

He shared with me his idea to bring a team of healthcare providers to help children with special medical needs. At that time I was the director of a public hospital in the city, and immediately we planned for them to come. They came and performed the surgeries. I believe the Lord used His servants to bring happiness to people in need. It was a blessing to see pastor Danny ministering to the parents of the children. The Christian hospital personnel were so touched they started a prayer group.

Right now I'm preparing to serve the Lord by studying the Word while waiting, in obedience and subjection for the Lord's timing to begin full time ministry."

Footprints - Alvaro Andrade

Africa Cape Verde

Dear Pastor Danny,

From far away in Africa, I want to thank you for your love, friendship, and leadership through all these years. While we worked together, I saw a man of God in you. You invested a lot in me. I am a blessed man today.

It was not necessary to open the Bible, make a theory or new theology, just to share time with my dear Pastor Danny, to feel his heart and his wife's love for one to be blessed. Thank you very much for everything you did for me (besides the cheese and ham rolls we shared in the mornings while we were even hungrier to share at the CVC radio station). You will always be a special person for Valeria and me.

When you want to eat a good fish under the moonlight, come to our home in South Africa."

Footprints - Angela Delfina Sierra

Ebenezer School Principal

One of the greatest blessings of my life is Pastor Danny Morales and his wife. In his years as a missionary among us, he was distinguished by his charisma, good humor, and above all his faithfulness to God. Through his teachings, I have learned that the flame of love must be turned on in our hearts to guide those in the darkness to find God.

I will never forget his words of consolation and encouragement when I was in great tribulation in the ministry of the Ebenezer School. The school was struck by a strong wind from Satan and was about to be closed by the government. Pastor Danny came from the United States to provide support when we needed it most. As a school principal, I have no words to thank this man of God for all his love, help, and the support he shared with the school staff and children. It was a joy for us when we received a call from the pastor announcing that he'd gotten some materials, desks, and equipment for the school. Thank you, Pastor Danny.

Footprints - Francisca Galo-Suazo

San Pedro Sula, Honduras

When I was a baby, my legs were accidentally burned. I was living in a remote village on a mountain without any hope. But I wanted to study, and I crawled to the elementary school for six years.

When my father heard on the radio that a medical team was coming to Comayagua, Honduras, he took me early in the morning to the health center, but I was told to return to the village because there was no hope for me. The team couldn't do that kind of surgery. On my way out, I met Pastor Danny, who asked me to come back to see the doctors.

As I crawled, the people moved away and let me pass by. Then Dr. Laurence Arnold saw me, and with heartfelt compassion, he said to Pastor Danny, "Let's take this girl to the United States to help her."

My parents agreed to send me to Florida with Pastor Danny, who helped me get a passport. A month later, he picked me up and took me to live with his family in Florida, where I stayed for the duration of the surgical procedure. The night before my surgery, he led me to receive Jesus in my heart.

After a painful surgery and therapy, I got my prosthetic legs, and I was able to walk for the first time in twenty-two years. I went back to Honduras walking, and I was able to stand by my mother and give her a hug. Pastor Danny found me a place to stay in San Pedro Sula, the loving home of Pastor Nehemías and his wife, Fanny, who adopted me as a daughter. He asked Dr. Tom and Susan, a couple from Florida, to sponsor my education. I finished middle school and high school, and now I am working on my thesis to get my college degree.

My life has changed. Now I can walk, and I am a college girl! I am very thankful to God, Brother Danny, Dr. Laurence Arnold, and Holy Cross Hospital and their staff for the donation of surgery and physical therapy. I also want to thank Dr. Tom and his wife as well as Nehemías and Fanny Chavarría for their support.

Thank you, Pastor Danny. Your footprints changed my life forever!

Footprints - Pastor Clelia Castillo

Avance Misionero

I thank God for giving me a special pastor, Danny Morales. Through his immense love for the Lord and his total dedication to the ministry, I learned how to be a servant. He left a deep mark on my heart and my spiritual life. I am currently a pastor of a beautiful congregation of one hundred members in Comayagua. It is my prayer and desire that every member of my congregation be mentored as I was by Pastor Danny.

Footprints - Diana Orellana

Avance Misionero Church, La Paz, Honduras

I thank the Lord for Pastor Danny's love and work for Honduras. I was so blessed when he brought a medical team to Comayagua. At that time, I was able to meet Dr. Laurence Arnold, God's servant, who arranged for my face surgery in Florida so that I would be able to smile. I am very thankful to God and Dr. Arnold. After the two surgeries, my life changed completely. Now I am in my last year of college and working as a teacher.

Pastor Danny asked Brother Jack Graham to help me. He donated the money to build me a house. I was touched when Pastor Danny adopted me as a daughter. He is always watching over me.

Chapter 12: Thank You, Dad

You had given me so much love and support. I give thanks to the Lord for giving us so much time to be together. Now that I am away from you, I miss you so much, and you know that I have to call every day to hear your voice. I have seen your faith, love, and compassion in your heart for the lost, the hurt, and the broken-hearted. Your passion to work for the Lord has impacted me. You taught me it is worthy to be faithful and to obey His call to serve, no matter what.

I want to follow your steps and reach many people with God's Word, living a life consecrated to God, the family, and the ministry as you have done all these years. Your faith has blessed me in the most difficult times of my life. I really appreciate you for giving me wise advice at the appropriate time and for your shoulder to lean on at the most difficult times. Thanks for always being by my side, listening, laughing, and praying. I have seen God's hand upon you.

Thank you for the plastic Big Wheels, the toy that I will never forget. You and Mom gave us the best. I know about the sacrifices you made so I would be able to study at a Christian College. Thanks. I hope that you will be happy and proud that I want to follow in your footsteps, serving God and raising my kids in the Lord as you have taught me. I hope that one day Victoria and David will embrace the ministry that God has for them like you did.

Thank you being such a great example for your children and grandchildren. I am a blessed daughter, so proud of having you as my father. Thank you, Dad, for being the best father, Rebecca.

From Frances Beatriz

Thank you, Daddy, for loving me the way you do, for being at my side in difficult times. I'll never forget the time you told me I was an angel, and I said, "Yes, but I can't fly." Thank you for loving my boys the way you do. They love to say in Spanish, "Te amo."

I give thanks to God because you are my father. You have given us a good example so we may love and serve God. Maybe I haven't expressed to you that you have a special place in my heart and I love you so much.

From Daniel Isaías

Dad, I still remember the special gift. You carried a small toy fire truck on your back at the flea market. Sweaty and tired, you got home with your surprise for your little boy (me), who wanted to be a firefighter at that time. Thank you, Dad. It was a nice and special surprise and a memory that I will keep in my heart. Today, I am a sheriff's deputy in Tuscaloosa, Alabama, and I am so proud to tell everybody that my father is a pastor and missionary.

Dad, thank you for your love, care, advice, and the support you've given me through the years. I have never lacked your blessing. I learned to be a good father and husband and serve God with your testimony. Thank you again for your advice and support. I have a grand example to follow.

From Liza Raquel

Dad, thank you for your love and blessing. I know that I may count on you, even if I am far away. I would like to thank you for keeping the binoculars that I gave you when I was a little girl. I still remember that I didn't have money to buy you a gift and that I got the idea of making a pair of binoculars using empty toilet paper rolls. You received it like it was an expensive gift and kept it.

Daddy, I admire your faith and love for the ministry. Thank you for the support, good advice, and encouragement at difficult times.

Liza sent the following letter on his birthday in January 25, 2010:

Dear Dad,

Happy Birthday! We love you!

Today is your birthday. May God bless you and continue to bless you always. I really wish we could be there to share your special day with you, but since we are so far away, I decided to write you this letter and tell you what is in my heart.

Daddy, when I think about you, about who you are and what you stand for, I can't help but feel such pride and admiration toward you. God has used you in so many ways to reach so many people because you have such a beautiful servant's heart. I am so proud to say that I am your daughter.

Dad, I want to take this time to thank you for all the hard work you and Mom went through, all the sacrifices you made to raise us in a happy home. Thank you for giving up buying yourself things (which I know both you and Mom did) in order to make sure you had enough money to feed and dress the four of us. Thank you for teaching me the importance of saving money and spending it wisely. Thank you to you and Mom for raising us in a home where Christ was the center, with strong values and principles that I can pass down to my own children.

My dear father, I want you to know that I am truly blessed to have you in my life. I thank God because He gave me the opportunity, honor, and privilege of serving you while you were broken and sick. Thank you for allowing me to nurse you back to health. Those moments we shared were special to me. It was an honor and a blessing that brought me great joy—knowing that I was serving a man of God, my father. And I know no matter what you say, no one can take as good care of you as I do—well, except for God and maybe Mom. Now as much as I liked taking care of you, I'd much rather you were healthy, sound, and happy.

Love always, your baby,

Liza Raquel

PS: At least you got a letter this time and not a blue toilet paper "thingy" Ha! Ha!

Hey, that was the best I could do at that age.

Chapter 13: You Will Leave More Footprints

Those who go out weeping, carrying seed to sow, will return with songs of joy, carrying sheaves with them.

—Psalm 126:6

My dearest husband, you have fulfilled your calling to preach but your work for the Lord is not finished. Your obedience to this call has reached hundreds of lives. During your forty-year walk sowing the seed of God's Word, you have wept, suffered, and endured many trials. And now, I wish for you to see the fruit of your obedience, which has inspired many to continue or begin working for the Lord.

Forty years after you embraced your call to preach, I see your hands full of sheaves. One day, you will be able to return with songs of joy to place beautiful fruit at the feet of the Master who called you. It is glorious to know that this story does not end here. Danny, I firmly believe that God holds you in the ranks of the courageous men of this millennium and you will still leave many more footprints.

God has shown His faithfulness and support for the call that He made to you to preach His gospel around the world. It is my prayer that you will continue leaving footprints were ever you go.

Your loving wife, Frances

Appendix 1

The following letter was sent to Danny by one of the "Guerrilla" members. This young man attended a Bible study in the city of San Pedro Sula, Honduras. While Danny preached, the Lord touched him and he accepted Jesus Christ as his Savior.

Consider this translation of the guerrilla's letter to Danny:

Beloved Brother Danny,

I greet you in the name of the Almighty.

Daddy, this is your son, Fernando, the "Guerrilla". I accepted Christ on August 7, 1971, after one of your messages. Do you remember?

I always remember you, and I would like to see you one of these days. I hope that God keeps using you always. God has magnified His mercy in allowing me to be part of His ministry. I am crucified with Him, and He lives in me.

I wish you and Frances many blessings in your ministry.

Many hugs from your spiritual son,

Fernando Alvarado, the "Guerrilla"

Appendix 2

Hymn Glory of Obedience

I have walked many roads, mountains,

And valleys, and I can't see greater glory,

Than the glory of obedience

There is no greater commandment on Earth,

The joy that floods the soul of God

It does not exist in heaven or on earth,

A greater glory, than to obey

Chorus

Glory, glory, glory without equal, does not exist for me.

Glory, glory, glory what a joy is living in His will.

I declare to the winds,

"I am God's property,

Nothing happens in my life without Him," who ordained it

All the time I love and enjoy God's order.

His glory is my life, His glory overpowers me and I live to obey.

Soon the Son, King of kings will appear,

To seek His beloved bride that awaits for Him.

That day the Church will join Him

And together they will rejoice.

They will sing praises for forever.

Pastor and missionary of Ramón Nieves

Appendix 3

A song to remember

God's comfort arrives when we need it the most. One day, Danny was in need of comfort and he received the lyrics of this song, he was encouraged and comforted by the loving words of this great friend. The following lyrics are from a song written by Pastor Sammy Johnson titled "Marks of a Friend". Pastor Johnson dedicated this song to Danny as a token of gratitude.

Marks of a Friend

As you go through your days of struggle and of time

There's much to remember oh friend of mine

Every step you took was on the high road

A model of integrity was your honor code

You always had the time to listen and advise

A word of encouragement lead me toward the prize

An attitude of gratefulness, a heart for what is true

A man of unmatched dignity in all you say and do

You have given to my life

More than you will know

You have impacted me

And now it finally shows

Smarter, wiser, kinder

Maybe a joke or two

You see if I've got the marks

Of a great friend

And that friend is you

Seldom do relationships ever stay the same

It seems someone's always in a state of change

But if you can make just one good friend in time

That's enough to last forever oh friend of mine

Sammy Johnson

*Danny, Judith and Gabriel leaving
for Honduras on July 12, 1970*

Danny and Frances Morales

Our Family

Granddaughters, Sofia, Victoria and Natalia

Ebenezer School

Ebenezer School Annex

Danny and Carlos Armenteros recording a radio program